GYMNASTICS

Gymnastics Skills

BEGINNING TUMBLING

by Jen Jones

Consultant
Connie Dickson
Minnesota State Chair
USA Gymnastics Women's Program

Capstone
press

Mankato, Minnesota

Snap Books are published by Capstone Press,
151 Good Counsel Drive, P.O. Box 669, Mankato, Minnesota 56002.
www.capstonepress.com

Library of Congress Cataloging-in-Publication Data
Jones, Jen.
Gymnastics skills : beginning tumbling / by Jen Jones.
p. cm. — (Snap books. Gymnastics)
Summary: "A guide for children and pre-teens on basic tumbling skills
needed for gymnastics"—Provided by publisher.
Includes bibliographical references and index.
ISBN-13: 978-0-7368-6470-1 (hardcover)
ISBN-10: 0-7368-6470-9 (hardcover)
1. Gymnastics—Juvenile literature. I. Title. II. Series.
GV461.3.J67 2007
796.44—dc22   2006002806

Editor: Wendy Dieker
Designer: Jennifer Bergstrom
Photo Researcher/Photo Editor: Kelly Garvin

Photo Credits:
Capstone Press/Karon Dubke, cover, 3 (middle, bottom), 4–5, 8, 11, 12–13 (both),
        16–17 (all), 20–21, 23 (all), 24–25 (both), 26 (all), 27
Jennifer Jones, 32
Masterfile/Brian Pieters, 18–19
PhotoEdit Inc./Frank Siteman, 3 (top), 6–7, 9
SportsChrome Inc./Michael Zito, 14–15, 29

Capstone Press thanks the staff and gymnasts at Rising Stars Gymnastics Academy
in Oakdale, Minnesota, for their assistance with photo shoots.

1 2 3 4 5 6 11 10 09 08 07 06

TABLE OF CONTENTS

6-7

20-21

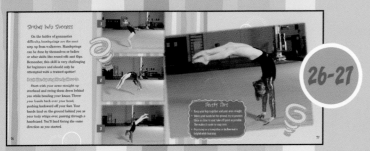

26-27

Features

Simply the Best

Advancing in gymnastics is like climbing a ladder.

You can't reach the top without putting in the work! In gymnastics, there are no shortcuts. As a beginner, you'll start out with simple skills. These skills are the rungs that lead to complicated stunts that are learned at the top.

This book will focus on perfecting basic gymnastic **techniques**, including rolls, cartwheels, round-offs, walkovers, and handsprings. We'll also discuss safety, training, and how to choose a gym that fits your needs. If each skill is a rung on the ladder to success, there's nowhere to go but up!

CHAPTER 1

Getting off the Ground

Secrets of Success

The best gymnasts move elegantly and gracefully. They make gymnastics look easy. In reality, gymnasts spend many, many hours training. A runner focuses on building **endurance** and speed. A dancer must develop grace and flexibility. However, a gymnast must excel in *all* of these areas. Then she needs to add **coordination**, body control, and balance to her skills. Gymnastics is truly a challenging sport!

You have to start somewhere! Gymnasts start by training safely at a good gym.

All of these factors come into play in different ways for each gymnastics event. For instance, on the balance beam, gymnasts must be in control. On the uneven bars, gymnasts need strength. For the vault, speed and power are key. During the floor exercise, gymnasts call on their dance and tumbling abilities. They also need endurance to make it through their routines.

Playing It Safe

Football players wear helmets and pads. Boxers use mouth guards and gloves. So what do gymnasts have to protect themselves from injury? Protective gear like **grips** and wrist guards help. Yet in gymnastics, the responsibility for your safety lies largely on your own shoulders. That's why paying attention to proper technique and practicing on a mat is so important!

Although this book provides instruction, it is meant to be used with in-person gymnastics classes. In class, your coach or **spotter** will work with you closely to perfect your moves. Never try a new skill without a trained professional present. You could seriously hurt yourself and be sidelined for good. No gymnast wants that!

"Other people may not have had high expectations for me, but I had high expectations for myself."

–Shannon Miller, U.S. Olympic medalist

Training Ground

When getting started, it's a smart idea to find a local program where you can take lessons. Gymnastics clubs are available in many cities and offer something for everyone from beginners to top-level competitors. The following checklist includes things to consider when choosing a gym.

Classes Does the club offer classes for your age and skill level? Are several levels of training offered so that you can grow and improve? Does the gym offer coaching for competition?

Building Is the space large enough to hold several groups of gymnasts practicing at once? What equipment does the gym have? How often is the equipment inspected for safety?

Instructors How experienced are the gym's instructors? Are they trained in gymnastics safety? How many students does each instructor teach at once?

To make sure a gym or club is right for you, ask if you can watch a class before joining. You wouldn't buy a dress without trying it on. So don't be afraid to take your gym for a trial run before signing up!

You're Getting Warmer

Starting a gymnastics workout without first warming up is like playing hockey without pads. It's important to take at least 15 minutes before any gymnastics workout to stretch out your muscles. Stretching cuts down on the risk of hurting yourself and improves your flexibility. Activities like jogging or jumping jacks will also get your blood flowing.

Turn up your body heat and start your workout with these surefire stretches.

Runner's Lunge

With your body in push-up position, bring your left foot forward between your hands. Keeping your hands on the ground, lean into the lunge. Hold the stretch for 10 seconds. Repeat with the other leg.

Bridge

While lying on your back, place your hands on the ground by your head with elbows in the air. Push your body upward while straightening your arms and legs. Your stomach and hips should be highest in the air, forming an upside-down U shape with your body. Hold the stretch for 10 seconds.

Just the Basics

Even the best gymnasts started with the basics covered in this chapter!

POWER POSITIONS

Your body twists and bends in many ways to form the shapes you see in gymnastics. Yet just a handful of positions form the basis for each move. Let's go over some of the basic body positions.

A lunge is a standing position. One leg is slightly bent in front of your body, and the other leg is straightened behind your body. Your body weight shifts onto the front leg.

A squat is a crouched sitting-type position in which your legs are bent and your bottom is lowered toward the ground.

Tuck

In **pike** position, your legs and arms are held straight in front of you and your toes are pointed.

In a **layout**, your arms are raised above your head so that your body looks like it's in a straight line.

A **tuck** is just that—your head is tucked inward and your knees and thighs are tucked in toward your chest.

On a Roll

Ready to roll like a rock star? Forward and backward rolls are little sisters to flips. They involve making a full body circle on the ground. Rolls are usually performed on the floor or the balance beam.

Forward Roll Handy How-To

Lower yourself to squat position with arms out in front of you, and bend forward. Tuck your head toward your chest, and put your hands on either side of your head. Push off with your feet and roll forward with legs bent, returning to squat position.

Take a Stand

If you don't stand for something, you'll fall for anything! Headstands and handstands are used in every gymnastics event, from the vault to the balance beam to the uneven bars to floor exercise.

Handstand Handy How-To

Starting in lunge position, lower both palms to the mat in front of you. Kick your back leg up, followed by your front leg. Both legs should meet in the air so your body forms a straight line. After holding the pose for several seconds, step down in the same direction or lower into a forward roll.

Trusty Tips

- You can practice against a wall or by kicking your legs up then quickly lowering to get the feel for the movement.

- Strengthening exercises, such as push-ups, will prepare your arms for supporting your body weight.

- Headstands are a great practice tool for learning handstands.

"We all must try to be the best person we can: by making the best choices, by making the most of the talents we've been given."

–Mary Lou Retton, U.S. Olympic medalist

Go Carting

Ready to do some wheelin' and dealin'? A cartwheel is a beginner-level skill. It acts as a stepping-stone to harder moves like round-offs and walkovers.

Cartwheel Handy How-To

For a left-sided cartwheel, stand in lunge position with your left leg in front and your arms overhead. Bend forward and lift your right leg as your left hand touches the ground. As your right hand touches the ground, your left leg will follow into the air, and you will be in handstand position. As your feet land one by one in lunge position, raise your hands overhead.

Trusty Tips

- Keep your body straight and your toes pointed.
- Imagine a straight line that you start and finish on; try not to veer off track!
- Remember this motto: "hand, hand, foot, foot."
- Your body should look like an X in mid-cartwheel.

3 Fundamentals to Flip Over

Once you master rolls and cartwheels, get ready to start flipping!

Round and Round We Go

Round-offs are like powerful cartwheels. They are designed to boost your body into back handsprings and flips.

Round-off Handy How-To

Often entered into with a running start or several fast steps, round-offs are very similar to cartwheels. The difference is that, in the middle of a round-off, your feet come together and your body does a half-twist. On the landing, your feet snap down together, and you end up facing the opposite direction.

TRUSTY TIPS

- Both round-offs and cartwheels can be done on either side of your body.
- After your feet land together, raise your arms overhead and jump into the air. This is good practice for pushing off into handsprings and other skills.

Walking the Walk

It's time to experience the wonder of walkovers! Forward and back walkovers are simple to perform and can be done on the floor or the beam. They also are good preparation for learning the motion of handsprings.

Back Walkover Handy How-To

Lift one leg as your body bends backward into bridge position. Your top leg should be straight, while the bottom leg is bent. Shifting your weight onto your hands, push off the ground with your bottom leg as your top leg heads toward the floor. Land in lunge position, with arms raised in victory!

Trusty Tips

- Look over your head toward the floor while bending backward.
- Practicing with a foam barrel is helpful while learning.

More Trusty Tips

- Keep toes pointed as you "walk over."
- Your legs should look like they're almost in the splits while in the air.

SPRING INTO SUCCESS

On the ladder of gymnastics difficulty, handsprings are the next step up from walkovers. Handsprings can be done by themselves or before or after skills like round-offs and flips. Remember, this skill is very challenging for beginners and should only be attempted with a trained spotter!

Back Handspring Handy How-To

Start with your arms straight up overhead and swing them down behind you while bending your knees. Throw your hands back over your head, pushing backward off your feet. Your hands land on the ground behind you as your body whips over, passing through a handstand. You'll land facing the same direction as you started.

1

2

3

Trusty Tips

- Keep your legs together and your arms straight.
- When your hands hit the ground, try to position them as close to your take-off point as possible. This makes it easier to snap over.
- Practicing on a trampoline or **incline mat** is helpful while learning.

Looking into the Future

Throughout the book, we've built a solid foundation for moving out of beginner-land and into the big leagues. The next step up on the ladder from a handspring is to learn flips, which are full 360-degree somersaults in the air.

Flips can be done with your body in many positions ranging from layout to tuck. They are often seen during the floor exercise. For a sneak peek at some advanced flips, look no farther than the handy cheat sheet on the next page.

"Every single element, even the most hair-raising, can be improved."

—Dmitry Bilozerchev, Russian Olympic medalist

Full Twist

Twist and shout as your body twists and turns in this corkscrew-style skill.

Pike Arabian

You'll flip for this funky flip, which combines elements of forward and backward somersaults in pike position.

Full-In

Double your fun in a double flip with a full twist added on the first rotation.

Full Twist

Glossary

coordination (koh-OR-duh-nay-shun)—the ability to control body movements

endurance (en-DUR-uhnss)—the ability to handle long periods of exercise

grips (GRIPS)—pieces of leather that gymnasts wear like gloves to protect the palms of the hands; grips help gymnasts hold onto the bars better.

incline mat (IN-kline MAT)—a mat shaped like a long triangle that is used for learning new gymnastics skills

spotter (SPOT-tur)—a trained professional that watches and helps gymnasts for safety reasons

technique (tek-NEEK)—the method or way of doing a certain skill

Fast Facts

C'mon, baby, let's do the twist!

In July 2005, American gymnast Nastia Liukin raised the bar. She became the first woman to perform a quadruple twist in competition at the U.S. Classic.

Your Name Here

New combinations of basic positions and skills are often named after the gymnasts who made them famous. For example, the Yurchenko twist is named after Russian gymnast Natalia Yurchenko.

Women Rock!

Females dominate gymnastics. According to USA Gymnastics, there were 62,646 women gymnasts in 2004. Only 12,076 gymnasts were male.

Read More

Bragg, Linda Wallenberg. *Play-by-Play Gymnastics.* Play-by-Play. Minneapolis: Lerner, 2000.

Herran, Joe, and Ron Thomas. *Gymnastics.* Action Sports. Philadelphia: Chelsea House, 2004.

Hughes, Morgan. *Gymnastics.* Junior Sports. Vero Beach, Fla.: Rourke, 2005.

Kalman, Bobbie, and John Crossingham. *Gymnastics in Action.* Sports in Action. New York: Crabtree, 2003.

Porter, David. *Winning Gymnastics for Girls.* New York: Facts on File, 2004.

Internet Sites

FactHound offers a safe, fun way to find Internet sites related to this book. All of the sites on FactHound have been researched by our staff.

Here's how:

1. Visit *www.facthound.com*

2. Choose your grade level.

3. Type in this book ID **0736864709** for age-appropriate sites. You may also browse subjects by clicking on letters, or by clicking on pictures and words.

4. Click on the **Fetch It** button.

Facthound will fetch the best sites for you!

About the Author

Jen Jones has been very involved in the cheerleading and gymnastics worlds since she was old enough to turn a cartwheel! Jen has several years of gymnastics training and spent seven years as a cheerleader. After college, Jen cheered and choreographed for the Chicago Lawmen semi-professional football dance team. Today Jen lives in Los Angeles and writes for publications like *Pilates Style*, *American Cheerleader*, and *Dance Spirit*. She also teaches cheerleading and dance classes and is a certified BalleCore instructor.

Index